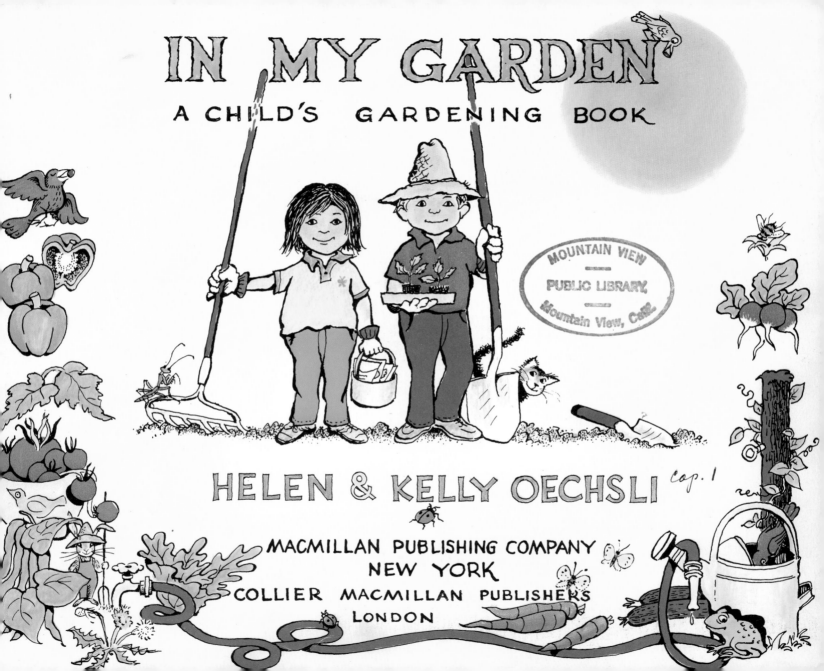

IN MY GARDEN
A CHILD'S GARDENING BOOK

HELEN & KELLY OECHSLI

MACMILLAN PUBLISHING COMPANY
NEW YORK
COLLIER MACMILLAN PUBLISHERS
LONDON

To Heidi

Library of Congress Cataloging in Publication Data: Oechsli, Helen. In my garden. Summary: A general guide to beginning gardening, with specific instructions for growing beans, carrots, lettuce, peppers, and other vegetables. 1. Vegetable gardening—Juvenile literature. [1. Vegetable gardening. 2. Gardening] I. Oechsli, Kelly, ill. II. Title.   SB324.O35 1985 635 84-21285 ISBN 0-02-768510-1

In My Garden

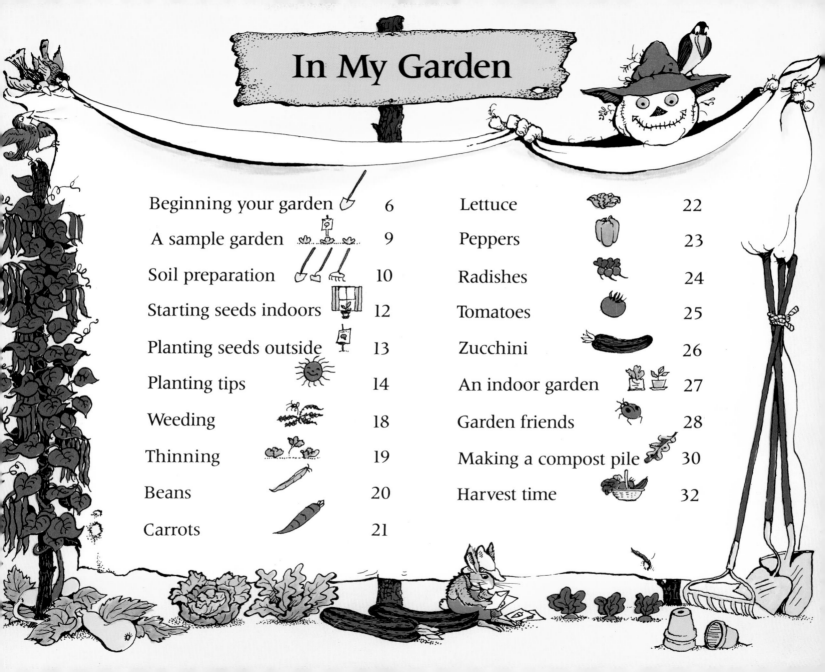

Have you ever tasted a home-grown tomato, or an ear of corn that was cooked a few minutes after it was picked?
You can.

Growing and eating some of your own food is a treat, and there are vegetables that will grow almost anywhere. Beans, radishes, and tomatoes are a few.

To begin your garden, find a good spot in your yard or community plot, or on a window sill. You want as much sun as you can get.

Remember that in the summer, when their leaves are full, trees will make shade. Most plants need direct sunlight to grow.

7

RADISH LETTUCE CARROT BUSH BEANS PEPPERS TOMATOES POLE BEANS

Some plants grow taller than others, and they also make shade. Be sure to place plants that grow tall, like tomatoes, so that they will not shade other vegetables.

GIVE EACH PLANT ENOUGH ROOM FOR IT TO BECOME FULLY GROWN

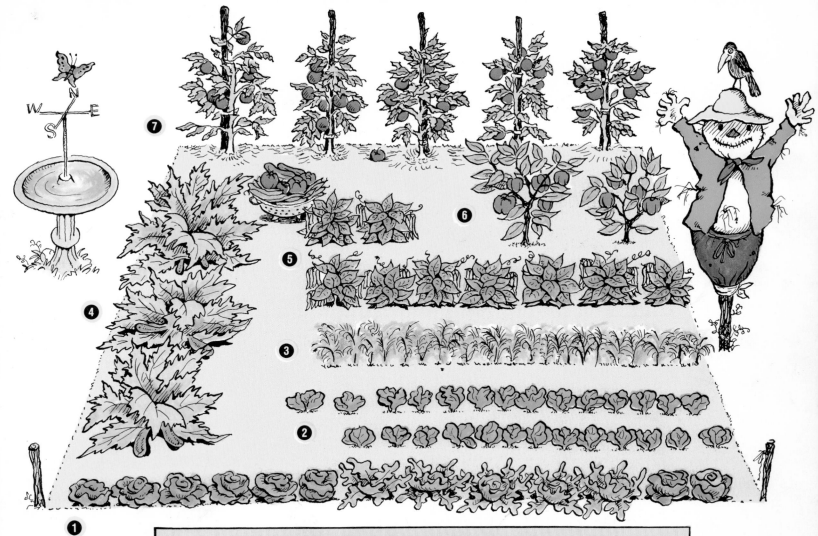

Here is a garden 10 feet wide by 12 feet long.

1. Lettuce   3. Carrots   5. Beans   7. Tomatoes
2. Radishes   4. Zucchini   6. Peppers

9

The time to start your garden depends upon the weather and the condition of the soil. If the ground is too wet, the dirt will stick to your shovel. Wait a few days or until the soil is dry enough to crumble in your hand.

Dig up the entire area of the garden and spread it with fertilizer. Fertilizer is the food that your plants will need to grow. Work it in with a hoe as you break up clumps of soil.

Finally, smooth the area with a rake. Your garden is ready for planting.

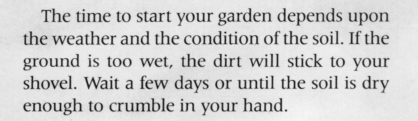

Only a few tools are needed.

ALWAYS PLACE TOOLS
WITH EDGES DOWN
FOR SAFETY!!

Watch a seed grow into a tomato!

 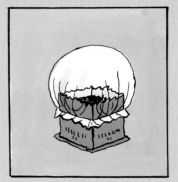  

April   May

   In the middle of April, plant a few tomato seeds in a small container that has been filled with soil.

   Moisten the soil, cover the container loosely with a piece of plastic wrap, and hold the wrap in place with a rubber band. Keep the container in a warm place. You have made a small greenhouse!

   When the seeds have grown into plants 1½ inches tall, remove the plastic and pull out all but the biggest plant. Being very careful, cut off a bottom corner of the container and set the container in a dish. Place it in a sunny window and water the plant from the bottom.

   After all danger of frost is over, put the plant out in the sun for several days, but be sure to bring it in each night.

June

July

August

By late spring your tomato plant will be ready to move to the garden. Gently removing the container, bury the plant so that the cube of soil is well covered. To keep it upright, use old pieces of cloth to tie the plant to a stick set firmly in the soil.

Over the next six weeks, you can watch the yellow blossoms develop into big, red, juicy tomatoes.

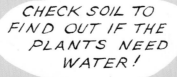

CHECK SOIL TO FIND OUT IF THE PLANTS NEED WATER!

Here are some planting tips.

• If you cannot start tomatoes and peppers indoors, you can buy small plants and put them in your garden. They may droop a little when first planted. Don't worry—they just need extra water for a day or two.

   Most other vegetable seeds can be planted directly into your garden.

- Before planting seeds, if the soil is very dry, sprinkle the garden with water but don't soak it. Then get ready to sow, or scatter, the seeds in a straight line.

STRINGS AND STICKS WILL MAKE THE ROWS STRAIGHT

- Seed packets will tell you how deep to plant. Pour some seeds in the palm of one hand, and sow them with the other. Do not scatter them too thickly, or the plants will not have room to grow.

- Pat the dirt over the seeds and sprinkle them lightly with water. The soil should be moist but not soaked.

Weeding

Don't forget to weed your garden. Weeds are plants that take away food and water that your vegetables need. After a rain, the garden can be hoed, and the weeds can be pulled easily.

ANYTHING NOT GROWING IN THAT STRAIGHT LINE YOU PLANTED YOU CAN BET WILL BE A WEED!

RADISH

Thinning

When your seeds begin to grow, they will be crowded. Since it's important to allow room for a plant's roots to spread out, you should pull out some of your seedlings to make space for others to grow. It's always hard to pull out what you've planted yourself, but later you'll be glad you did.

DON'T BE TIMID ABOUT THINNING.

19

These are favorite vegetables to grow:

Beans

Easy to plant, easy to grow, easy to pick, beans are popular with all gardeners. Beans can be eaten raw, or they can be cooked, canned, or frozen.

Plant beans when all danger of frost is over. Pole beans grow on vines that need long poles for support. Place the poles (or long sticks) in the ground far enough apart so the plants will not shade other vegetables. Plant seeds around each pole.

Bush beans are low plants and can be grown anywhere.

POLE BEANS 65 DAYS
BUSH BEANS 50 DAYS

Carrots

Carrots are a big favorite. They can be planted early in the spring. Plant some every three weeks and you will have a fresh supply through summer and into winter. Carrots take a long time to come up, so be patient and water the seeds regularly. Thin the plants well so that they can grow to the right size. Pulled out early, carrots are small and very tasty in salads.

Lettuce

All gardens should have lettuce. Lettuce grows best in cool weather and can be planted early in spring. In the heat of summer, lettuce grows well in partial shade. Plant some in late summer for fresh lettuce during the fall.

Thin the lettuce when it is about three or four inches high. At this size the thinnings are easy to replant elsewhere in the garden. Be sure to water the replanted lettuce well for several days.

Loose-leaf lettuces are good vegetables for home growing. The leaves can be pulled off as they are used, or the entire lettuce can be pulled.

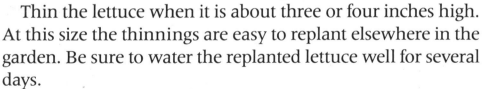

Peppers

Pepper plants are attractive. They can be grown in many places—in large pots near the porch, in front of a house as decorative bushes, or in rows in the garden.

Since peppers take a long time to grow, it is easiest to buy small pepper plants at the nursery and plant them in your garden in late spring. When the peppers are deep green and turning red, they are fully ripe and sweet.

70 DAYS

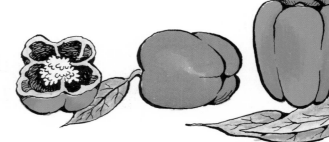

Radishes

Radishes are the fastest-growing crop of them all. Some ripen in twenty to thirty days, so only plant a few at a time. When radishes are the size of large marbles, they should be eaten. At that time the leaves are tender and can be added to salads.

Radishes can be planted in many out-of-the-way places in the garden. They like cool weather and can be planted early in the spring, as soon as the soil can be worked.

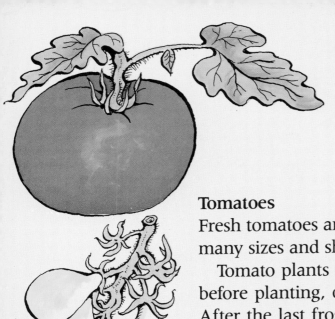

Tomatoes

Fresh tomatoes are the gardener's delight. Tomatoes come in many sizes and shapes, and all are delicious.

Tomato plants may be started at home six to eight weeks before planting, or they may be purchased from a nursery. After the last frost, put the small plants a bit deeper in the ground than they had been growing in their pots. Roots will grow from the stems that are underground.

Like pole beans, tomato plants need to be staked. Put stakes in place when you plant, so you won't disturb the plants later on. When the tomato plants are about fifteen inches high, tie them to the stakes.

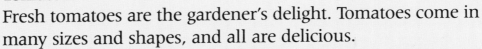

Zucchini (summer squash)

Be ready for surprises with zucchini. It grows with great speed and as soon as the leaves get large, bright yellow flowers start popping out. Check these blossoms every few days. The zucchini grow behind the flowers, and they are best for eating when about nine inches long. Picking zucchini makes room for new zucchini to grow.

Plant zucchini seeds when all danger of frost is past. Thin the plants so that they are about twenty-four inches apart.

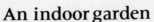

An indoor garden

Many plants can be grown indoors. Good vegetable plants for your sunny window sill are cherry tomatoes and green peppers. They can be grown in pots that are only six inches high.

Also try lettuce, baby carrots, and radishes.

Be sure to make holes in the bottoms of your containers for good drainage. Too much water will drown your indoor plants.

Bluebird

Some friends of the garden that help to keep out pests:

Praying Mantis

Lady Bug

Hawk

Brown Thrasher

Oriole

Woodpecker

Owl

Black-and-White
Warbler

Flicker

Wasp

Toad

Starling

What do you do with old weeds? What do you do with all of those lawn clippings and leaves that you raked in the fall?

YOU CAN USE ALL OF THESE IN YOUR GARDEN NEXT YEAR...

IF YOU START A COMPOST PILE.

Making a compost pile

Place all your grass clippings, leaves, weeds, coffee grounds, eggshells, and any other kitchen leftovers—except meat or oil—in a pile in a corner of your garden.

Keep the top of the pile slanted toward the center to catch the rain. Moisture helps this mixture to change its form. You are helping nature make rich new soil for next year's garden.

cap. 1

At last, everything is ripe and wonderful tasting! The seeds and tiny plants started in the spring have become a rich autumn harvest in your garden.